Karyashree – Believe and Achieve

OrangeBooks Publication

Smriti Nagar, Bhilai, Chhattisgarh - 490020

Website: **www.orangebooks.in**

First Edition, 2023

GRATITUDE.......THOUGHTS AND FEELINGS......ACTION

KARYASHREE

BELIEVE AND ACHIEVE

BY SANDIGDHA MISHRA

Orange Books Publication

www.orangebooks.in

Preface

"KARYASHREE" is a non-fiction book that delves into the profound impact of a parent's belief in their child. As you navigate through the pages of this book, you will discover numerous fascinating facts and elements that may resonate with your own experiences.

This book has been a labor of love, and we are confident that it will strike a chord with its readers. Whether you are a casual reader or an avid book lover, we hope you will find something special within the pages of "KARYASHREE".

It emphasizes the idea that when you believe in your child's abilities (Karya), their potential for success knows no bounds (Shree).

Sandigdha is a devoted professional who is focused on enhancing child education and rural development to create a positive impact on the lives of both children and communities. She is an advocate by profession and has done her masters in commerce and certification courses in child psychology, child protection framework, cognitive behavior therapy, and Neuro-Linguistic programming from esteemed institutions such as Harvard University. She has acquired the necessary knowledge and expertise to effectively address the challenges faced by children in various areas. Having worked in the education sector for over a decade, she possesses valuable insights into these challenges, which have fuelled her passion to seek solutions that help children reach their full potential.

She is a child protectionist and a Life Coach for children and adolescents; she is deeply committed to aiding the younger generation in acquiring the essential abilities required for success in life. Her primary areas of focus are resilience, emotional intelligence, and self-esteem, and she works closely with young people to assist them in surmounting obstacles and accomplishing their aspirations. By employing a blend of mentorship, coaching, and skill-enhancement exercises, she supports the development of children and adolescents' self-confidence and resilience, empowering them to flourish in today's rapidly changing world.

A Note from the Author………………

In 2008, I married my dream man, and we made a deliberate choice to meticulously evaluate the repercussions of all the decisions we took as we were pursuing CA together. Right from the beginning, we agreed to prioritize our education, establish our careers, and achieve financial stability before planning for a family so that we could provide the best possible life for our child. After being married for almost seven years, in December 2014, we were blessed with KARYASHREE, who brought us an immense amount of happiness. The moment I held her for the first time, I was filled with tears of happiness as I looked into her expressive face, her beautiful eyes, and her tiny hands and feet. It was the most extraordinary moment of my life. Our families were thrilled as well and celebrated the arrival of the first grandchild on both sides. It is pertinent to mention that during our dating phase, we had already made up our minds about wanting a daughter as our first child, and I had even chosen the name Karyashree, which fit her perfectly.

Although there were some difficulties along the way, my baby girl had to be admitted to NICU for two days due to her low birth weight of 2.2 kg. Unfortunately, her weight dropped even further to 1.8 kg in the following days, causing a stressful and difficult fifteen-day period for me as a new mother.

In addition to the challenges in caring for my new-born baby girl, I had to deal with harsh criticism and judgment from my in-laws and my own family. Specifically, the statements like I am an incompetent mother who did not know how to properly feed and care for her child was the harshest one. That only added to my stress and made it even more difficult for me to navigate the challenges of motherhood.

As a first-time mom, I faced numerous challenges in even the most basic tasks, and I wished they could have understood my lack of experience and shown me some empathy.

Despite all the drama, I refused to give up, and I eventually learned to successfully breastfeed my child. Despite my ongoing struggle, I encountered further challenges in persuading my daughter to eat properly, and I faced criticism from friends and family for it. My daughter was a thin, tiny girl, and I felt like I was failing as a mother because I couldn't make her gain weight. But I understood that the judgments and criticism were simply a result of my family's overprotectiveness towards my daughter, who was the first child in the family, causing them to overlook the difficulties I was facing. Looking back, though, I realize that Karyashree was trying to reassure me during those difficult nights and days, reminding me that we were both fighters and we could overcome any challenges.

Subsequently, as she grew up, everyone in the neighborhood, family, relatives, and even my friends had a single assessment that this child is very skinny; how she will manage, survive, or how unfortunate her situation is etc... But I always knew that my daughter was strong and resilient from day one. And this belief was proven when Karyashree accomplished a significant achievement by winning a silver medal at the National Taekwondo Championship in the year - 2022 at the age of 7.

The achievement of my daughter serves as evidence that her strength and resilience, coupled with my beliefs, have played a significant role in her success.

Currently, Karyashree is 8 years old, and I continue to hold the same belief today. I see my daughter as a fighter, a warrior, an intelligent and unique individual, a top-tier dancer and performer, an inventor, an artist, and the list goes on. However, my unwavering belief in her capabilities means that she can achieve anything.

Her name, Karyashree, signifies that whatever task she undertakes (the Karya), she will excel at it (Shree).

My intention with this book is to encourage all parents to have faith in their children's abilities, allowing them to soar high and reach for the skies.

"This book aims to outline the techniques, strategies, and approaches I use to achieve my goals, in the hope that they may be helpful to you and your children."

Thank you!

Content

Introduction:

As parents, we have a profound impact on our children's growth and development. Our beliefs, values, and attitudes shape the way we interact with our children and the world around us. But did you know that our beliefs can also have a significant impact on our children's growth and development? In this book, we will explore the power of beliefs and how they can affect our children's growth. We will also provide practical strategies to help parents develop positive beliefs that can positively impact their children's growth and development.

Parents play a significant role in shaping their children's growth and development. One way in which parents can influence their children's growth is through their beliefs. Here are some ways in which parents' beliefs can impact their children's growth:

- **Beliefs about intelligence and ability**: Parents' beliefs about their children's intelligence and abilities can affect how they view their children's potential. Children, who are praised for their efforts and encouraged to develop their skills and talents, are more likely to have a growth mindset and believe that they can improve through hard work and dedication. Conversely, children who are told that their intelligence or ability is fixed may be more likely to have a fixed mindset and believe that their abilities are predetermined and cannot be changed.

- **Beliefs about discipline:** Parents who believe in using harsh punishment to discipline their children may be more likely to have children who fear punishment rather than learning from their mistakes. On the other hand, parents who use positive reinforcement and emphasize the importance of learning from mistakes may have children who are more willing to take risks and learn from their experiences.

- **Beliefs about gender roles:** Parents who hold traditional beliefs about gender roles may be more likely to encourage their children to conform to gender stereotypes. For example, they may encourage boys to be aggressive and assertive while discouraging girls from being assertive or taking on leadership roles. These beliefs can limit children's growth and development and prevent them from exploring their full potential.

- **Beliefs about education:** Parents who value education and believe in its importance may be more likely to encourage their children to do well in school and pursue higher education. Conversely, parents who do not value education may not prioritize their children's academic success, which can limit their opportunities and potential.

In summary, parents' beliefs can have a profound impact on their children's growth and development. By being mindful of their beliefs and how they communicate them to their children, parents can help their children reach their full potential and develop into well-rounded individuals.

For instance, a parent who strongly believes that academic achievement is the key to success may push their child to excel in their school by providing extra academic support, enrolling them in advanced courses, or pressuring them to study harder. As a result, the child may develop a strong work ethic, a sense of discipline, and an appreciation for learning.

On the other hand, a parent who believes that success is primarily determined by social skills and networking may encourage their child to focus on building relationships and developing social skills. This could lead the child to prioritize extracurricular activities, such as sports, drama, or music, which provide opportunities to develop social skills and build networks.

In both cases, the parent's beliefs are likely to shape the child's attitudes and behaviors, which in turn can have a significant impact on their future success and happiness. It's important for parents to be aware of their own beliefs and how they may be influencing their children's development, and to be open to different approaches that may be more appropriate for their children's individual needs and interests.

Parents play a crucial role in shaping their child's attitudes and behaviors. As children grow and develop, they observe and learn from their parents' actions, beliefs, and values. This process is known as socialization, and it can have a profound impact on a children's future.

One-way, parents influence their child's attitudes and behaviors through their beliefs. Parents hold a variety of beliefs about the world, including beliefs about religion, politics, and morality. These beliefs can shape a child's worldview and affect how they approach different situations in life.

For example, if a parent strongly believes in the value of honesty, they may teach their child to always tell the truth, even in difficult situations. This can influence the child's behavior and attitude towards honesty, making them more likely to prioritize telling the truth in their own lives.

Similarly, if a parent holds strong political beliefs, they may teach their child to support the same political party or ideology. This can shape the child's attitudes towards different issues and influence their behavior in the future, such as how they vote or what causes they support.

Parental beliefs can also influence a child's attitudes towards religion. If a parent is religious, they may teach their child to follow the same religion and instill in them the values and beliefs associated with that religion. This can shape the child's worldview and affect their behavior in various ways, such as how they interact with people of different religions or how they approach moral issues.

It's important to note that parental beliefs are not the only factor that shapes a child's attitudes and behaviors. Other factors, such as peers, teachers, and the media, also play the role. However, parents have a unique and powerful influence over their child's development, particularly in the early years of life.

In conclusion, parental beliefs are likely to shape a child's attitudes and behaviors. By instilling their values and beliefs in their children, parents can shape their child's worldview and influence their behavior in various ways. Therefore, it's important for parents to be mindful of their beliefs, and how they may affect their child's development.

Similarly, children's beliefs are a crucial part of their development and can have a significant impact on their attitudes and behaviors. As children grow and learn, they develop their own beliefs about the world around them, which are influenced by a variety of factors, including their family, culture, and experiences.

One way, children's beliefs can shape their attitudes and behaviors, is through their perceptions of themselves and others. For example, if a child believes that they are not good at sports, they may avoid participating in physical activities or feel discouraged when playing with their peers. This can affect their self-esteem and behavior in the future, such as their willingness to try new things or their level of confidence in themselves.

Similarly, children's beliefs about others can affect their attitudes and behaviors towards them. If a child believes that people from different cultures or backgrounds are inferior, they may be less likely to interact with them or treat them with respect. This can lead to prejudice and discrimination, which can have negative consequences for both the child and those around them.

Children's beliefs about morality and values can also shape their attitudes and behaviors. If a child believes that honesty and kindness are important, they may be more likely to behave in ways that reflect those values. On the other hand, if a child believes that lying and cheating are acceptable, they may engage in those behaviors without considering the consequences.

It's important to note that children's beliefs are not set in stone and can change over time. As children gain new experiences and information, they may adjust their beliefs and attitudes accordingly. Therefore, it's essential to provide children with diverse experiences and exposure to different perspectives to help broaden their beliefs and understanding of the world.

In conclusion, everyone's beliefs are likely to shape their attitudes and behaviors. By understanding the impact of their beliefs, parents, caregivers, and educators can help children develop positive beliefs and values that will serve them well in the future. Encouraging critical thinking, exposure to diverse experiences, and positive role models can all contribute to shaping children's beliefs in positive ways.

Chapter 1

WHAT ARE
BELIEFS AND WHY ARE THEY
IMPORTANT?

This chapter will define beliefs and explain why they are essential in shaping our children's growth and development. It will also explore the different types of beliefs that we hold and how they can impact our lives and the lives of our children.

"Your beliefs affect your choices. Your choices shape your actions. Your actions determine your results. The future you create depends upon the choices you make and the actions you take today."

*— **Roy T. Bennett***

eliefs are ideas or concepts that we hold to be true, regardless of whether they are supported by evidence or not. They can be shaped by a variety of factors, including culture, family, religion, and personal experiences. Beliefs can be very powerful and can have a significant impact on our thoughts, emotions, and behavior.

When it comes to shaping our kids, our beliefs can have a major influence on their development and worldview. Children are very impressionable, and they often adopt the beliefs of their parents and caregivers. This can include beliefs about everything from religion and politics to values and social norms.

However, it is important to recognize that not all beliefs are beneficial or accurate. Parents who hold beliefs that are harmful, discriminatory, or inaccurate may inadvertently pass these beliefs on to their children, which can have negative consequences for their development and well - being.

In summary, beliefs are powerful ideas that can shape our thinking, emotions, and behavior. As parents and caregivers, it is important to be mindful of the beliefs we hold and the impact they may have on our children.

Let's understand beliefs and impacts:

Positive beliefs are thoughts or assumptions that people hold about themselves, others, or the world around them that are optimistic, empowering, and eventually comes true. Here's an example:

Positive belief: "I can achieve my goals."

Impact: This belief can have a significant positive impact on a person's life. It can motivate and direct them to take action towards achieving their goals, even in the face of obstacles and setbacks. It can help them develop a growth mindset, which is essential for learning and personal development. It can also help them build self-confidence and resilience, which are important qualities for success in any area of life.

Overall, positive beliefs can have a profound effect on a person's mental health, well-being, and success. By cultivating positive beliefs and challenging negative ones, individuals can improve their outlook on life and achieve their full potential.

Let's understand beliefs and impacts:

Similarly, negative beliefs are thoughts or assumptions that people hold about themselves, others, or the world around them that are pessimistic, limiting, and often untrue. Here's an example:

Negative belief: "I'm not good enough."

Impact: This belief can have a significant negative impact on a person's life. They may avoid taking risks or trying new things, believing they will inevitably fail. They may struggle with low self-esteem and self-worth, leading to feelings of sadness and depression. They may also find it difficult to form meaningful relationships, as they believe they are not worthy of love or attention.

Overall, negative beliefs can be very damaging to a person's mental health and well-being. It's important to identify and challenge these beliefs in order to overcome them and live a more positive and fulfilling life.

While challenges may still arise, your beliefs shape your actions and ultimately manifest into your reality. This is not to say that obstacles will never appear, but rather that your mindset plays a crucial role in how you approach and overcome them.

Beliefs are an integral part of every person's life, including children. What children believe about themselves and the world around them can have a profound impact on their choices, actions, and ultimately their reality.

It is very important to understand that Children's beliefs are shaped by their experiences, interactions with others, and the messages they receive from the world around them. These beliefs can either support or hinder their personal growth and development.

For example, if a child believes that they are capable of achieving their goals and dreams, they are more likely to take action towards achieving them. On the other hand, if a child believes that they are not good enough, they may avoid taking risks and miss out on opportunities for growth and development.

Similarly, a child's beliefs about other people can also impact their actions and choices. If a child believes that people are generally kind and trustworthy, they are more likely to develop positive relationships and seek out new friendships. Conversely, if a child believes that people are mean or untrustworthy, they may struggle to develop healthy relationships and miss out on opportunities for social growth and development.

It's essential for parents, caregivers, and educators to understand the power of children's beliefs and work to cultivate positive and empowering beliefs in children. This can be achieved by providing children with positive feedback, offering opportunities for growth and development, and encouraging them to take risks and explore their interests.

For example, if a child is interested in art, parents can encourage them to pursue this interest by providing them with art supplies, enrolling them in art classes, and displaying their artwork around the house. This reinforces the child's belief in their ability to create and succeed in the field of art.

It's also important to be mindful of the message's children receive from media, peers, and society at large. Negative messages can create limiting beliefs that hinder children's growth and development. For example, messages about gender roles and stereotypes can limit a child's belief in their ability to succeed in certain fields or pursue certain interests.

In conclusion, children's beliefs have a significant impact on their actions and choices, which ultimately shape their reality. By cultivating positive and empowering beliefs in children, we can help them achieve their full potential and create a brighter future for themselves and those around them.

THE IMPACT OF LIMITING BELIEFS ON CHILDREN'S GROWTH

This chapter will examine the negative impact of limiting beliefs on children's growth and development. It will explore how negative beliefs can affect a child's self-esteem, confidence, and ability to achieve their goals. The chapter will also provide examples of common limiting beliefs that parents may hold and how they can work to overcome them.

"Courage is your natural setting. You do not need to become courageous, but rather peel back the layers of self-protective, limiting beliefs that keep you small."

*— **Vironika Tugaleva***

L imiting beliefs can have a significant impact on a child's growth and development. Children learn and internalize beliefs about themselves and the world around them from a young age, often through interactions with parents, caregivers, and other adults.

When children are exposed to limiting beliefs, such as "I'm not good enough," or "I'll never be able to do that," it can have a negative impact on their self-esteem and confidence. These beliefs can become deeply ingrained and affect a child's ability to learn, take risks, and grow.

For example, if a child believes they are not good at math, they may be less likely to try challenging math problems or pursue careers that require strong math skills. Similarly, if a child believes that success is only achievable through natural talent, they may be less likely to put in the effort required to develop skills and achieve their goals.

Limiting beliefs can also lead to a fixed mindset, where a child believes that their abilities and traits are fixed and unchangeable. This can be detrimental to their growth and development, as it limits their potential and ability to learn new things.

Therefore, it is important for parents, caregivers, and educators to be aware of the impact of limiting beliefs on children and work to promote positive beliefs and attitudes. Encouraging a growth mindset, emphasizing effort and hard work, and providing opportunities for children to develop and explore their strengths can help counteract the effects of limiting beliefs and promote healthy growth and development.

Parents, it is important to keep in mind that once limiting beliefs are identified, it is essential to encourage your child to question their beliefs and understand why they think the way they do. It would be helpful to help them recognize their strengths and abilities and show them evidence that disproves their limiting beliefs.

Another way to combat limiting beliefs is to expose the child to positive role models. These can be individuals who have overcome similar challenges or achieved success despite facing obstacles. Seeing someone who has achieved their goals despite facing similar limiting beliefs can be a powerful motivator for a child.

Finally, it is essential to create a positive and supportive environment for the child. Encourage them to try new things, take on challenges, and celebrate their successes. Offer praise and recognition for their efforts, regardless of the outcome. Encouraging a growth mindset, where failure is seen, as an opportunity to learn and grow, can also help to combat limiting beliefs.

In conclusion, children are exposed to limiting beliefs in various forms and ways. It' is essential to identify these beliefs, challenge them, expose children to positive role models, and create a positive and supportive environment to combat them. By doing so, children can develop a growth mindset and achieve their full potential.

Chapter 3

THE POWER
OF POSITIVE BELIEFS ON
CHILDREN'S GROWTH

In this chapter, we will explore the positive impact of beliefs on children's growth and development. We will examine the importance of positive self-beliefs, growth mindset, and resilience in promoting a child's success. The chapter will also provide practical strategies to help parents develop positive beliefs in their children.

"Create a positive space around you, even if it's in your mind. You must have an environment of good energy in order to give that."

— Anonymous

Positive beliefs can have a significant impact on a child's growth and development. When children believe in themselves and their abilities, they are more likely to take risks, try new things, and persevere through challenges. This can lead to a sense of accomplishment and build self-esteem, which can further motivate them to continue learning and growing.

Research has shown that parents and caregivers play a crucial role in shaping children's beliefs about themselves and the world around them. When parents provide positive feedback, offer encouragement, and model a growth mindset, children are more likely to develop positive beliefs about their abilities and potential.

Positive beliefs can also have a long-term impact on a child's success in life. Children who have positive beliefs about their abilities are more likely to set high goals for themselves, work hard to achieve them, and have a greater sense of control over their lives. This can lead to improved academic performance, better social relationships, and greater overall well- being.

In summary, fostering positive beliefs in children is crucial for their growth and development. Parents and caregivers can play a key role in this process by providing positive feedback, encouragement, and modelling a growth mindset. By instilling positive beliefs in children from an early age, we can help them reach their full potential and achieve success in life.

Some positive beliefs for the child's growth:

- ❖ "I believe that every child has unique strengths and talents, and with the right support and encouragement, they can achieve anything they set their mind to."

- ❖ "I believe that every child has the potential to learn and grow, and the mistakes and challenges are opportunities for them to develop resilience and problem-solving skills."

- ❖ "I believe that children are inherently curious and motivated to explore and discover the world around them, and that as being parents and caregivers, we can foster their natural curiosity and creativity."

❖ "I believe that every child has the ability to develop strong social and emotional skills, and that by nurturing their relationships with others and providing them with a safe and supportive environment, we can help them become kind, empathetic, and confident individuals."

❖ "I believe that children thrive when they feel loved and valued, and that by providing them with positive feedback and celebrating their achievements, we can help them develop a strong sense of self -esteem and self-worth."

Positive beliefs are essential to a child's growth and development. They foster a sense of self-worth, resilience, motivation, and social skills that ultimately lead to a positive outcome. Positive beliefs are a powerful tool that parents, caregivers, and educators can use to help children thrive.

Self-Worth

Positive beliefs help children develop a healthy sense of self-worth. When children believe in themselves, they are more likely to take on challenges and succeed. Children who have positive beliefs are more likely to see themselves as capable, competent, and valuable. This sense of self - worth can carry over into all areas of their lives, including academics, athletics, and social interactions.

Resilience

Positive beliefs also help children develop resilience. When children believe they can overcome obstacles, they are more likely to persevere in the face of adversity. Children who have positive beliefs are better able to cope with stress, setbacks, and disappointments. They are more likely to bounce back from difficult situations and emerge stronger and more confident.

Motivation

Positive beliefs can also motivate children to achieve their goals. When children believe they can succeed, they are more likely to put in the effort necessary to achieve their goals. Positive beliefs can help children develop a growth mindset, where they see challenges as opportunities to learn and grow. Children with positive beliefs are more likely to set goals, work hard, and achieve success.

Social Skills

Positive beliefs can also contribute to the development of social skills. Children who believe in themselves are more likely to be confident in social situations. They are more likely to initiate conversations, make friends, and develop positive relationships. Children with positive beliefs are also more likely to show empathy, kindness, and respect for others.

Positive Outcomes

Ultimately, positive beliefs can lead to positive outcomes for children. Children who have positive beliefs are more likely to be happy, healthy, and successful. They are more likely to achieve their goals, develop positive relationships, and have a positive outlook on life. Positive beliefs can set children on a path toward a bright and promising future.

Conclusion

Positive beliefs can contribute significantly to a child's growth and development. They foster qualities such as self-worth, resilience, motivation, and social skills that ultimately lead to a positive outcome. Parents, caregivers, and educators can help children develop positive beliefs by providing them with positive feedback, setting realistic goals, and encouraging them to take on challenges. By fostering positive beliefs in children, we can help them reach their full potential and achieve success in all areas of their lives.

Chapter 4

HOW TO FOSTER POSITIVE BELIEFS IN OUR CHILDREN

This chapter will provide practical strategies for parents to foster positive beliefs in their children. It will examine the role of praise, encouragement, and positive reinforcement in promoting positive beliefs. The chapter will also explore the importance of modelling positive beliefs and attitudes in promoting positive beliefs in our children.

"Don't let what you can't do stop you from doing what you can do."

— John Wooden

Fostering positive beliefs in children is an important part of their development, as these beliefs can shape their self-esteem, sense of purpose and overall well-being. Here are some tips to help you encourage positive beliefs in your children:

- **Encourage self-awareness:** Help your child to understand their strengths, weaknesses, and interests. This will help them develop a sense of self-awareness and confidence in their abilities.

- **Provide positive feedback:** Offer specific and genuine praise when your child does something well. This will help them to feel good about themselves and their abilities.

- **Model positive beliefs:** Children often model the behavior of their parents, so it's important to model positive beliefs for yourself. Talk positively about yourself and others and avoid negative self-talk or criticism.

- **Encourage resilience:** Teach your child to bounce back from setbacks and failures. Help them understand that mistakes are a natural part of the learning process and that they can use their failures as opportunities for growth and development.

- **Encourage a growth mindset:** Help your child to develop a growth mindset by emphasizing the importance of effort and hard work rather than innate talent or intelligence. Encourage them to take risks and try new things.

- **Teach gratitude:** Help your child to appreciate what they have by emphasizing gratitude. Encourage them to focus on the positive aspects of their life and to express gratitude regularly.

- **Encourage positive self-talk:** Teach your child to talk to themselves in a positive and encouraging way. Encourage them to use affirmations or positive statements to reinforce their positive beliefs.

Parents play a critical role in shaping their child's beliefs and attitudes. Fostering positive beliefs in children is an ongoing process that requires consistent effort and dedication. It is not something that can be achieved overnight, but rather, it is a continuous journey that requires patience and perseverance.

One of the most important aspects of fostering positive beliefs in children is to keep the lines of communication open. It is essential to have open and honest conversations with your child and listen to their thoughts and feelings. By doing so, you can gain a better understanding of what is going on in their lives and provide them with the support they need.

Creating a supportive environment is also crucial when it comes to fostering positive beliefs in children. Children thrive when they feel safe, loved, and supported. As a parent, it is important to create an environment where your child feels comfortable and secure. This can be achieved by providing a stable home life, setting clear boundaries, and offering consistent praise and encouragement.

Reinforcing positive behaviors and beliefs is another essential component of fostering positive beliefs in children. When your child exhibits positive behaviors or beliefs, it is important to acknowledge and praise them. This can be done through verbal affirmation, physical gestures, or even rewards. By doing so, you reinforce positive behaviors and beliefs, and your child is more likely to continue exhibiting them.

It is important to remember that fostering positive beliefs in your child is a long-term process. It requires patience, dedication, and consistency. However, the benefits of fostering positive beliefs in your child are immeasurable.

By doing so, you are setting your child up for success and helping them to become confident, resilient, and happy individuals.

Chapter 5

OVERCOMING NEGATIVE BELIEFS AS A PARENT

In this chapter, we will explore how parents can overcome their own negative beliefs that may be impacting their children's growth and development. We will examine the role of self-awareness, self-reflection, and seeking support in overcoming negative beliefs.

"We can lift ourselves, and others as well, when we refuse to remain in the realm of negative thought and cultivate within our hearts an attitude of gratitude."

–Thomas S. Monson

O vercoming negative beliefs as a parent can be a challenging process, but it is important for your personal well-being and your child's growth and development.

Here are some tips that may help:

- **Identify your negative beliefs:** Start by recognizing the negative beliefs that you have about yourself as a parent. It could be beliefs like "I'm not good enough," "I'm too strict," "I'm not patient enough," or "I'm too lenient." Once you identify these beliefs, you can begin to challenge them.

- **Challenge negative beliefs:** Question the negative beliefs that you have identified by asking yourself whether they are actually true. Look for evidence that supports or contradicts these beliefs. Consider alternative perspectives and ask yourself whether you would say the same things to someone else.

- **Reframe your negative beliefs:** Instead of thinking in terms of negative beliefs, try to reframe them into more positive and supportive thoughts. For example, if you believe that you are not patient enough, reframe that belief into "I am working on becoming more patient."

- **Practice self-compassion:** Be kind to yourself and treat yourself with the same understanding and compassion that you would offer to a close friend. Recognize that you are doing your best as a parent and that it is okay to make mistakes.

- **Seek support:** Talk to other parents, a therapist, or a coach who can help you identify and challenge your negative beliefs. They can provide an objective perspective and offer guidance and support.

Remember that overcoming negative beliefs as a parent is a process, and it may take time and effort. But by taking steps to challenge these beliefs and reframe them in a more positive light, you can become a more confident and effective parent.

As a child, I held certain beliefs about myself, such as that being a girl meant I was weak and unable to take care of myself due to my chronic illnesses. I thought I needed to rely on someone stronger than me for my safety.

Additionally, I believed that I was better at math than English. However, over time, through training, experience, and increased awareness, I was able to overcome these beliefs. I didn't want my child to have the same limiting beliefs that I once held, so I worked to change them and turn them into positive realities.

The process of self-evaluation is ongoing. Whenever we experience negative thoughts or fears, it's important to examine our belief system in order to reassess it. By doing so, we can then take the necessary steps to strategize and turn it into a positive experience with beneficial outcomes.

Sarah, a young woman, who struggled with anxiety and self-doubt. Sarah had always been a perfectionist and believed that anything less than perfection was a failure. She often found herself overwhelmed and paralyzed by fear, unable to take action or make decisions.

One day, Sarah decided to seek help from a coach. Gradually she learned about the importance of self-evaluation and began to examine her belief system. She realized that her belief that anything less than perfection was a failure was causing her anxiety and preventing her from taking action.

Sarah learned to challenge her negative thoughts and fears by examining the evidence and looking for alternative explanations. She also learned to reframe her thoughts and beliefs in a more positive light, focusing on her strengths and accomplishments rather than her failures and shortcomings.

Through this process of self-evaluation, Sarah was able to overcome her anxiety and self-doubt. She learned to accept herself for who she was and to embrace her imperfections. She also gained the confidence to take risks and pursue her goals, knowing that she was capable of handling whatever challenges came her way.

Sarah's story is a powerful example of the importance of self-evaluation. Whenever we experience negative thoughts or fears, it's important to examine our belief system in order to reassess it. By challenging our negative thoughts and reframing our beliefs in a more positive light, we can overcome our fears and achieve our goals. Self-evaluation is a powerful tool that can help us to become more self-aware, resilient, and confident individuals.

Chapter 6

WHY OUR BELIEFS AS PARENTS ARE IMPORTANT IN OUR CHILD'S GROWTH

The power of beliefs is undeniable. As parents, we have a significant responsibility to shape our children's growth and development positively. By developing positive beliefs, we can help our children reach their full potential and live fulfilling lives. This book has provided practical strategies to help parents develop positive beliefs in their children and overcome negative beliefs that may be impacting their children's growth and development. Remember, the beliefs we hold today will shape the future of our children tomorrow.

"A child is a beam of sunlight from the Infinite and Eternal, with possibilities of virtue and vice, but as yet unstained."

— Lyman Abbott

Our beliefs can have a significant impact on our child's growth and development in several ways:

- **Shaping their worldview:** Children learn a lot from their parents' beliefs and values. Our beliefs about the world, society, and people around us can shape our children's perceptions and understanding of these things.

- **Developing their moral compass:** Our beliefs about right and wrong, good and bad, just and unjust can help guide our children's moral development. Our actions and words based on those beliefs can teach them what is acceptable behavior and what is not.

- **Providing a sense of security:** Children often feel safe and secure when they have a clear understanding of what their parents believe in. It can give them a sense of stability and predictability in their lives.

- **Building their self-esteem:** When parents believe in their children's abilities and talents, it can help them develop a positive self-image and confidence in themselves.

- **Influencing their behavior:** Our beliefs and attitudes can affect our behavior, and children often model their behavior after their parents. If we have positive beliefs and attitudes, it can help our children develop positive behaviors.

Therefore, it's important to be mindful of our beliefs and how they may impact our children. As parents, we have a great responsibility to ensure that our beliefs are helping our children develop into confident, caring, and responsible individuals.

Let's take the example of a parent who wants to instill the value of empathy in their child. The parent may consciously model empathy by demonstrating kindness and understanding towards others, whether it is towards a friend or a stranger. They may also encourage their child to engage in acts of kindness, such as volunteering or donating to a charity.

The parent may also expose their child to diverse cultures and experiences by encouraging them to learn about and appreciate the perspectives of others. They may encourage their child to read books or watch movies that portray characters from different backgrounds and walks of life. The parent may also encourage their child to interact with people from different cultures and backgrounds, whether it is through community events or travel.

Additionally, the parent may send positive messages that reinforce the value of empathy. They may praise their child when they exhibit kindness and understanding towards others, emphasizing the importance of treating others with respect and dignity. The parent may also encourage their child to stand up for those who are marginalized or oppressed, helping them to develop a sense of social responsibility.

Overall, the parent's beliefs about the value of empathy are reflected in their actions, words, and interactions with their child. By consciously modelling and reinforcing positive beliefs, the parent is helping their child develop into a confident, caring, and responsible individual who understands the importance of treating others with kindness and respect.

Chapter 7

GROWTH MINDSET: THE POWER OF "YET"

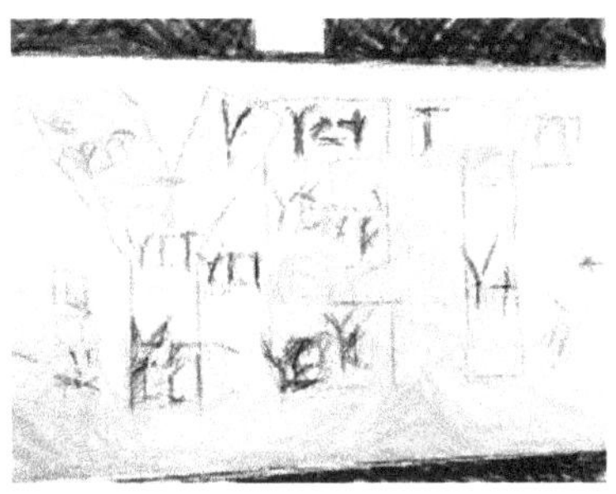

In this chapter, we will understand the mindset and impacts:

- *What is a growth mindset?*

- *How to develop a growth mindset in ourselves and our kids?*

- *Practical tips for fostering a growth mindset at home.*

"It never gets easier. You just get better."

— ***Jordan Hoechlin***

The concept of a growth mindset is based on the belief that intelligence and abilities can be developed through effort, learning, and persistence. A key component of this mindset is the power of the word "yet." When faced with a challenge or setback, individuals with a growth mindset will add "yet" to the end of their thoughts, such as "I haven't mastered this skill yet," or "I haven't figured this out yet."

By using "yet", individuals acknowledge that they may not have achieved their goals or overcome their obstacles, but they are not giving up. Instead, they are acknowledging that growth and development take time and effort. This mindset can help individuals stay motivated and persistent, even when faced with difficult tasks or setbacks.

Research has shown that individuals with a growth mindset are more likely to embrace challenges, persist through obstacles, and ultimately achieve their goals. On the other hand, those with a fixed mindset, who believe that intelligence and abilities are fixed and cannot be changed, are more likely to avoid challenges and give up in the face of setbacks.

Therefore, the power of "yet" is a crucial tool for developing a growth mindset and achieving personal and professional success. By embracing the idea that growth and development take time, effort, and persistence, individuals can cultivate a mindset that will help them overcome obstacles and achieve their goals.

For example, instead of saying, "I can't do this," which implies a fixed mindset and a belief that our abilities are limited, we can say, "I can't do this yet," which suggests that we are still learning and have the potential to improve. This shift in mindset can help us to stay motivated and persevere through challenges, knowing that we have the ability to grow and develop our skills over time.

By embracing the power of "yet," we can cultivate a growth mindset that allows us to approach challenges with a sense of optimism and a belief in our own potential. This can help us to achieve personal and professional success by allowing us to learn from our mistakes, persist through difficult times, and ultimately reach our goals.

Let's talk about Jack Andraka. Jack is a young scientist who developed a new method for detecting pancreatic cancer when he was just fifteen years old. Jack's discovery came after he had been rejected from multiple labs and had faced many setbacks in his research. Despite these obstacles, Jack maintained a growth mindset and continued to experiment and learn from his mistakes.

In an interview, Jack said that he believed that failure was simply a part of the learning process and that he needed to keep trying new things until he found what worked. Jack's growth mindset helped him to stay motivated and persevere through challenges, ultimately leading to his ground-breaking discovery. Today, Jack is an inspiration to many young people and a great example of the power of a growth mindset.

Chapter 8

OVERCOMI NG THE FIXED MINDSET:

This chapter will make us learn the following aspects:

- *Understanding the fixed mindset*

- *How to recognize fixed mindset thinking in ourselves and our kids*

- *Strategies for shifting from a fixed to a growth mindset*

"Most of the important things in the world have been accomplished by people who have kept on trying when there seemed no hope at all."

--Dale Carnegie

A fixed mindset is the belief that intelligence, abilities, and talent are innate and cannot be developed through effort and practice. People with a fixed mindset tend to avoid challenges, give up easily when faced with obstacles, and believe that failure is a reflection of their inherent ability.

If you want to overcome a fixed mindset, here are some strategies that can help:

Embrace a growth mindset:

In recent years, the concept of a growth mindset has become increasingly popular, and for good reason. A growth mindset is athe belief that our abilities and intelligence can be developed through hard work, dedication, and perseverance. It is the opposite of a fixed mindset, which assumes that our abilities and intelligence are predetermined and unchangeable.

Embracing a growth mindset can have a profound impact on our lives. When we believe that we can improve and develop our abilities through hard work and dedication, we become more motivated and engaged in the learning process. We are more likely to take on new challenges, persevere through difficulties, and ultimately achieve our goals.

One of the key aspects of a growth mindset is embracing the power of "yet". When we encounter a challenge or setback, we can remind ourselves that we haven't mastered it "yet". This simple shift in mindset can help us stay motivated and focused on our goals, even when progress is slow or setbacks occur.

Another important aspect of a growth mindset is the belief that failure is simply a part of the learning process. When we encounter failure, we can view it as an opportunity to learn and grow rather than a reflection of our abilities or worth. By embracing failure as a natural part of the learning process, we become more resilient and better equipped to handle challenges in the future.

So, how can we embrace a growth mindset in our own lives?

The first step is to become more aware of our own beliefs and self-talk. When we catch ourselves thinking in a fixed mindset, we can challenge those beliefs and remind ourselves of the power of growth and learning.

We can also focus on the process of learning, rather than just the end result. By setting goals that focus on growth and improvement rather than just achieving a certain outcome, we can stay motivated and engaged in the learning process.

Finally, we can surround ourselves with people who embrace a growth mindset. When we are part of a community that values hard work, dedication, and learning, we are more likely to adopt those values ourselves.

In conclusion, embracing a growth mindset can have a profound impact on our lives. By believing in the power of growth and learning, we can become more motivated, engaged, and resilient in the face of challenges. By challenging our fixed beliefs, focusing on the process of learning, and surrounding ourselves with like-minded individuals, we can cultivate a growth mindset that helps us achieve our goals and live our best lives.

View challenges as opportunities:

Challenges are an inevitable part of life. They can come in many forms- from a difficult project at work to a personal setback. However, it's important to remember that challenges are also opportunities for growth and learning. When we embrace challenges as a chance to develop new skills and expand our abilities, we can transform difficult situations into positive experiences.

One of the first steps in embracing challenges is to adopt a growth mindset. A growth mindset is the belief that our abilities and intelligence can be developed through hard work and dedication. When we have a growth mindset, we view challenges as opportunities to learn and grow rather than as threats to our abilities or worth.

Another important aspect of embracing challenges is to focus on the process rather than just the end result. When we focus on the process of learning and growth, we are more likely to stay motivated and engaged, even in the face of difficulty. We can break down a challenge into smaller and more manageable steps and focus on making progress every day.

It's also important to remember that challenges can be a chance to develop new skills and expand our abilities. When we encounter a challenge, we can ask ourselves what skills or abilities we need to develop in order to overcome it. We can seek out resources, such as books or courses, to help us learn new skills and techniques.

Finally, it's important to seek support when we face challenges. Whether it's from friends, family, or a mentor, having a support system can help us stay motivated and encouraged when we encounter difficulty. We can also seek out feedback and guidance from others who have faced similar challenges in the past.

In conclusion, challenges are opportunities for growth and learning. By embracing challenges as a chance to develop new skills and expand our abilities, we can transform difficult situations into positive experiences. By adopting a growth mindset, focusing on the process of learning process, seeking out new skills and abilities, and seeking support from others, we can overcome challenges and achieve our goals.

Learn from failure:

Failure is a part of life that we all experience at some point. It can be difficult and painful, but it's important to remember that failure is also an opportunity to learn and grow. When we view failure as a chance to identify areas where we can improve and develop new skills, we can turn a negative experience into a positive one.

One of the first steps in reframing failure is to recognize that it is not a reflection of our abilities or worth. Just because we fail at something does not mean that we are incompetent or incapable. Instead, we can view failure as a natural part of the learning process and an opportunity for growth.

Another important aspect of viewing failure as an opportunity is to take responsibility for our mistakes. It's easy to blame others or external factors for our failures, but it's more productive to examine our own actions and decisions. By taking responsibility for our mistakes, we can identify areas where we need to improve and develop new skills.

It's also important to approach failure with a growth mindset. Instead of viewing our abilities as fixed and unchangeable, we can adopt the belief that we can develop and improve through hard work and dedication. When we have a growth mindset, we are more likely to view failure as a chance to learn and grow rather than as a setback.

One way to learn from failure is to reflect on the experience and identify what went wrong. We can ask ourselves questions such as: What were the factors that led to the failure? What could I have done differently? What can I learn from this experience? By reflecting on our failures, we can identify areas where we need to improve and develop new skills.

Finally, it's important to use failure as a motivation to try again. Instead of giving up after a failure, we can use it as a reason to keep working and striving towards our goals. We can use the lessons we learned from our failures to develop new strategies and approaches and to continue growing and learning.

In conclusion, failure is an opportunity to learn and grow. Instead of viewing failure as a reflection of our abilities or worth, we can view it as a chance to identify areas where we can improve and develop new skills. By taking responsibility for our mistakes, approaching failure with a growth mindset, reflecting on our experiences, and using failure as a motivation to try again, we can turn failure into a positive and transformative experience.

Embrace feedback:

Feedback is an essential tool for growth and development. Whether we are trying to improve our skills in a particular area or seeking to become better leaders, feedback from others can help us identify our strengths and weaknesses and improve our performance.

The first step in seeking feedback is to identify people who can provide us with constructive criticism. These can be our colleagues, mentors, or trusted friends who are knowledgeable and experienced in the areas we want to improve. Once we have identified these individuals, we should approach them with a specific request for feedback. This can be in the form of a specific question or request for a critique of our performance.

It's important to approach feedback with an open mind and a willingness to learn. We should be prepared to hear both positive and negative feedback and should avoid becoming defensive or dismissive of criticism. Instead, we should view feedback as an opportunity to learn and improve.

One effective way to receive feedback is to ask for specific examples. For instance, if you're seeking feedback on your public speaking skills, you could ask for examples of times when you were particularly effective, as well as, instances when you could have improved. By providing specific examples, feedback providers can help us better understand our strengths and weaknesses and identify areas for improvement.

Once we have received feedback, it's important to take action on it. This may involve practicing new skills, seeking out additional training or resources, or working on specific behaviors or habits. By taking action on feedback, we can turn criticism into a valuable tool for growth and development.

Another important aspect of feedback is providing it to others. Just as we seek feedback from others, we should also be willing to provide constructive criticism to our colleagues and team members. By providing feedback in a respectful and constructive way, we can help others improve their skills and abilities and contribute to the overall success of the team.

In conclusion, feedback is a valuable tool for growth and development. By seeking out feedback from others, approaching it with an open mind, asking for specific examples, taking action on feedback, and providing feedback to others, we can improve our skills and abilities and achieve greater success in our personal and professional lives. So, always be open to feedback and use it to become the best version of yourself.

Let's say that you are a software developer who has been working on a new project for a few weeks. You feel like you have been making good progress and are confident in your abilities, but you know that there is always room for improvement.

To get some feedback on your work, you decide to reach out to a colleague who has more experience in software development than you havedo. You ask them to review your code and provide feedback on what you could do better.

Your colleague takes the time to review your work and provides you with some constructive criticism. They point out some areas where your code could be more efficient and suggest a few different approaches that you could try.

While it's not always easy to hear criticism, you take their feedback to heart and begin implementing their suggestions. Over time, you notice that your code is becoming more streamlined, and your projects are taking less time to complete. You also feel more confident in your abilities as a software developer.

Thanks to the feedback you received, you were able to identify areas where you could improve and develop new skills. As a result, you have become a more effective and efficient developer, and you are better equipped to tackle new challenges in the future.

Cultivate a learning mindset:

A learning mindset is a belief that no matter what stage of life you are in, you can always learn and grow. It's an attitude that embraces challenges and experiences as opportunities for personal and professional development.

People with a learning mindset believe that intelligence and abilities are not fixed traits, but rather can be developed over time. This belief is rooted in the idea of neuroplasticity, which is the brain's ability to change and adapt in response to new experiences and challenges.

To cultivate a learning mindset, it's important to develop a love of learning. This means seeking out new experiences, reading books and articles, attending workshops and conferences, and pursuing hobbies and interests that challenge you intellectually.

It's also important to embrace challenges as opportunities for growth. When faced with a difficult task or problem, people with a learning mindset don't shy away from it. Instead, they approach it with a sense of curiosity and a willingness to learn.

In order to maintain a learning mindset, it's important to be open to feedback and to view failure as an opportunity to learn and grow. When things don't go as planned, people with a learning mindset don't get discouraged. Instead, they reflect on what they could have done differently and how they can improve in the future.

Developing a learning mindset can have a profound impact on every aspect of your life. When you approach challenges and experiences with a sense of curiosity and a willingness to learn, you are more likely to be successful and to enjoy the process of learning and growing.

Moreover, having a learning mindset can help you develop resilience and cope with setbacks more effectively. When faced with adversity, people with a learning mindset don't give up. Instead, they see it as an opportunity to develop new skills and strategies.

In conclusion, cultivating a learning mindset is essential for personal and professional growth. By embracing challenges, pursuing new experiences, and viewing failure as an opportunity to learn, you can develop a love of learning that will serve you well throughout your life. So, always remember that you have the power to learn and grow and embrace new challenges and experiences as opportunities for personal and professional development.

By embracing a growth mindset, viewing challenges as opportunities, focusing on effort, learning from failure, embracing feedback, and cultivating a learning mindset, you can overcome a fixed mindset and achieve your goals.

A real-life example of a growth mindset can be seen in the story of Michael Jordan, the legendary basketball player. As a high school student, Jordan was cut from the varsity basketball team. Instead of letting this setback discourage him, he used it as motivation to work harder and improve his skills. He practiced every day, worked on his weaknesses, and eventually became one of the greatest basketball players of all time.

Jordan's growth mindset allowed him to overcome his initial fixed mindset, which had made him believe that he wasn't good enough to play on the varsity team. By embracing the idea that he could improve his skills through hard work and practice, he was able to achieve his goals and become a basketball icon.

This example shows that having a growth mindset can help individuals overcome obstacles and achieve their goals. By believing that their abilities can be developed through dedication and hard work, people can push themselves to reach their full potential and accomplish great things.

Chapter 9

THE IMPACT
OF POSITIVE SELF-TALK

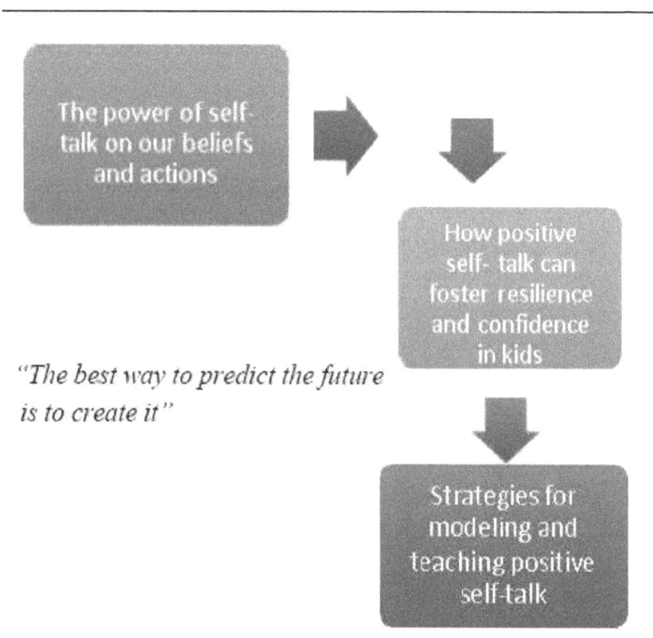

"The best way to predict the future is to create it"

Positive self-talk can have a significant impact on an individual's mental, emotional, and physical well-being. When we engage in positive self-talk, we replace negative or self-defeating thoughts with positive and empowering ones, which can lead to improved self-esteem, confidence, and overall well-being.

Research has shown that positive self-talk can help individuals better manage stress, reduce anxiety and depression symptoms, and even improve physical health outcomes. For example, athletes who engage in positive self-talk have been found to perform better and recover more quickly from injuries. Additionally, individuals who use positive self-talk in their daily lives report feeling more optimistic and happier overall.

When we engage in positive self-talk, we are essentially rewiring our brain to focus on more positive and empowering thoughts, which can help us overcome challenges and achieve our goals. It is important to note, however, that positive self-talk is not a one-size-fits-all solution and may not be effective for everyone. Some individuals may benefit from therapy or other forms of support to address underlying mental health concerns.

Overall, the impact of positive self-talk can be significant and can contribute to improved mental, emotional, and physical health outcomes.

Positive self-talk refers to the internal dialogue we have with ourselves and the messages we give ourselves about our abilities, worth, and potential. It's a way of nurturing a positive and supportive relationship with ourselves.

The impact of positive self-talk can be significant and can contribute to improved mental, emotional, and physical health outcomes.

Here are some ways in which positive self-talk can benefit us:

Improved self-esteem: Positive self-talk can help us build a more positive self-image, which in turn can lead to improved self-esteem. When we believe in ourselves and our abilities, we are more likely to take on new challenges and pursue our goals with confidence.

Reduced stress and anxiety: Negative self-talk can contribute to feelings of stress and anxiety, whereas positive self-talk can help to reduce these feelings. By replacing negative self-talk with positive and supportive messages, we can cultivate a sense of calm and relaxation.

Improved physical health: Research has shown that positive self-talk can have a positive impact on physical health outcomes. For example, it has been linked to reduced pain and improved immune function.

Increased motivation: When we use positive self-talk, we are more likely to feel motivated and energized. Positive self-talk can help us focus on our goals and overcome obstacles rather than giving in to self-doubt and negativity.

So, how can we cultivate positive self-talk? Here are some tips:

- **Be kind to yourself:** Treat yourself with the same kindness and compassion you would show to a friend.

- **Focus on the positive:** Instead of dwelling on your weaknesses or failures, focus on your strengths and accomplishments.

- **Practice gratitude:** Take time each day to reflect on the things you are grateful for and use this as a way to reinforce positive self-talk.

- **Challenge negative self-talk**: When you notice negative self-talk, challenge it with positive and supportive messages.

In conclusion, the impact of positive self-talk can be significant and can contribute to improved mental, emotional, and physical health outcomes. By cultivating a more positive and supportive relationship with ourselves, we can improve our self-esteem, reduce stress and anxiety, improve physical health, and increase motivation. So, next time you catch yourself engaging in negative self-talk, take a moment to replace it with a more positive and supportive message. Your mind and body will thank you for it.

Let's say the child is struggling with math and feels like she's not good at it. The parent could say, "I believe in you, and I know you can do it. You just need to keep practicing, and you'll get better." The child might respond with, "But I'm just not good at math." The parent could then say, "It's okay to struggle sometimes.

Everyone has subjects they find difficult, but that doesn't mean you can't improve. Remember that mistakes are opportunities to learn and grow."

As the child continues to practice and improve, the parent could provide further positive reinforcement, such as saying, "I'm so proud of you for working hard and not giving up. Look how much progress you've made!" The child might then start to believe in herself and her abilities and use positive self-talk to encourage herself when faced with challenges in the future.

By using positive self-talk, the parent is not only helping his/her child develop a growth mindset but also building a strong and supportive relationship with his/her son/daughter. This kind of positive reinforcement and encouragement can help the child to develop confidence, resilience, and a positive self-image, all of which can contribute to her overall growth and success.

Chapter 10

BUILDING CONFIDENCE THROUGH FAILURE

In this chapter we will understand:

- *The importance of failure in growth and learning*

- *How to help kids embrace failure and learn from it*

- *Strategies for building confidence through failure*

"We gain strength, and courage, and confidence by each experience in which we really stop to look fear in the face ... we must do that which we think we cannot."

–Eleanor Roosevelt

uilding confidence through failure is a process that involves self-reflection, resilience, and a growth mindset. Here are some steps you can take to build confidence through failure:

I. **Change your perception of failure:** Instead of seeing failure as a negative thing, reframe it as an opportunity for growth and learning. Understand that everyone fails at some point in their lives, and it's not a reflection of your self-worth.

II. **Set realistic goals:** Set achievable goals, and don't try to take on too much at once. This will help you build confidence as you achieve each goal.

III. **Take action:** Don't let the fear of failure hold you back. Take action and try new things. Even if you fail, you'll learn valuable lessons that will help you succeed in the future.

IV. **Learn from your mistakes:** When you experience failure, take the time to reflect on what went wrong and what you could do differently next time. Use this information to make adjustments and improve your chances of success in the future.

V. **Practice resilience:** Resilience is the ability to bounce back from setbacks. Practice resilience by staying positive and motivated, even in the face of failure. Remember that failure is not permanent, and you can always try again.

VI. **Celebrate small wins:** Recognize and celebrate your successes, no matter how small they may be. This will help you build confidence and keep you motivated.

VII. **Surround yourself with supportive people:** Surround yourself with people who believe in you and your abilities. Their encouragement and support will help you build confidence and overcome setbacks.

Remember, building confidence through failure is a process that takes time and effort. Stay committed to your goals and keep pushing forward, even in the face of adversity.

One real-life example of a great scientist building confidence through failure is the story of Marie Curie, a pioneer in the field of radioactivity.

Curie faced many obstacles in her career. She was a woman in a field dominated by men, and she had to fight for recognition and respect. She also struggled with financial difficulties and health issues.

Despite these challenges, Curie persisted in her research and made ground-breaking discoveries. However, she also faced setbacks and failures along the way, including the deaths of several colleagues and family members due to exposure to radiation.

Despite these setbacks, Curie continued to push forward and refine her methods. She learned from her mistakes and used her failures as opportunities to improve her research. Her perseverance and dedication ultimately led to her discovery of two new elements, polonium and radium, and earned her two Nobel Prizes.

Curie's story is a testament to the power of persistence and resilience in the face of failure. She did not let her setbacks defeat her but used them to build her confidence and push herself to new heights of scientific achievement.

Chapter 11

THE ROLE OF MINDFULNESS IN GROWTH

In this chapter, we get the awareness and the of:

- *Understanding mindfulness and its benefits.*

- *How mindfulness can help kids develop a growth mindset and resilience.*

- *Strategies for practicing mindfulness with kids.*

"Do every act of your life as though it were the very last act of your life."

— Marcus Aurelius,

Mindfulness can play a significant role in personal growth for both adults and children. It involves being fully present and aware of the present moment, without judgment or distraction. Here are some ways mindfulness can help with personal growth:

Reduced Stress and Anxiety: Mindfulness can help reduce stress and anxiety, allowing you to be more focused and productive.

In our fast-paced and often stressful world, it can be easy to become overwhelmed and anxious. The good news is that mindfulness practices can help reduce stress and anxiety, allow us to be more focused and productive.

Mindfulness is the practice of being present and fully engaged in the current moment. It involves paying attention to your thoughts, feelings, and bodily sensations without judgment. By practicing mindfulness, we can develop greater awareness, and control over our thoughts and emotions and learn to respond to them in a more constructive way.

Here are some ways in which mindfulness can help reduce stress and anxiety:

- **Reducing the impact of stress:** Mindfulness can help reduce the impact of stress on our bodies and minds. By becoming more aware of our stress triggers and learning to respond to them in a more positive way, we can reduce the physical and emotional toll that stress can take.

- **Improving focus and productivity:** When we are stressed and anxious, it can be difficult to focus on the task at hand. Mindfulness can help us stay focused on the present moment, allowing us to be more productive and efficient.

- **Increasing self-awareness:** Mindfulness practices can help us become more aware of our thoughts, feelings, and bodily sensations, allowing us to identify the sources of our stress and anxiety.

- **Promoting relaxation:** Mindfulness practices, such as deep breathing and body scan meditations, can help promote relaxation and reduce feelings of tension and anxiety.

So how can you incorporate mindfulness into your daily life? Here are some tips:

- **Start small:** Begin by incorporating short mindfulness practices into your daily routine, such as taking a few deep breaths before starting a task or taking a short mindfulness walk during your lunch break.

- **Practice regularly:** Consistency is the key when it comes to mindfulness. Try to practice mindfulness for a few minutes each day, gradually increasing the amount of time as you become more comfortable with the practice.

- **Use mindfulness apps:** There are a variety of mindfulness apps available that can help guide you through different mindfulness practices.

- **Be patient:** Mindfulness is a skill that takes time and practice to develop. Be patient with yourself and trust that the more you practice, the easier it will become.

In conclusion, mindfulness practices can help reduce stress and anxiety, allowing us to be more focused and productive. By incorporating mindfulness into our daily lives, we can improve our self-awareness, reduce the impact of stress, and promote relaxation. So, the next time you feel stressed or anxious, take a moment to practice mindfulness and see how it can benefit you.

Improved Mental Health: Mindfulness has been shown to improve mental health by reducing symptoms of depression and anxiety.

Mindfulness is a mental technique that involves paying attention to the present moment and accepting one's thoughts, feelings, and bodily sensations without judgment. Mindfulness-based interventions, such as mindfulness-based cognitive therapy (MBCT), have been shown to be effective in reducing symptoms of depression and anxiety in various studies.

The practice of mindfulness can help individuals with depression and anxiety by allowing them to observe their thoughts and emotions without becoming overly attached to or overwhelmed by them. This can help to reduce the negative impact of these thoughts and emotions on their mental state, leading to a decrease in symptoms.

In addition, mindfulness can help individuals to develop a greater sense of self - awareness and acceptance, which can help them to better cope with the challenges and stressors of everyday life. By becoming more present and aware, individuals may also develop a greater sense of resilience and emotional regulation, which can improve their overall mental health and well-being.

Overall, mindfulness can be a useful tool for managing symptoms of depression and anxiety and promoting overall mental health.

Increased Self-Awareness: Mindfulness can help you become more aware of your thoughts, emotions, and behaviors, allowing you to make positive changes in your life.

By practicing mindfulness, you can become more aware of your thoughts, emotions, and behaviors in a non-judgmental way. This increased awareness can help you to recognize patterns of negative thinking or behavior that may be holding you back or causing you distress.

For example, if you are prone to negative self-talk, mindfulness can help you to become more aware of these thoughts and to recognize them as patterns that may be contributing to feelings of low self- esteem or depression. Once you have identified these patterns, you can begin to challenge them and replace them with more positive and affirming self- talk.

Similarly, mindfulness can help you to become more aware of your emotions, allowing you to recognize when you are feeling anxious, stressed, or overwhelmed. By becoming more aware of these emotions, you can take steps to manage them in healthy ways, such as through relaxation techniques, exercise, or reaching out for social support.

Finally, mindfulness can help you to become more aware of your behaviors, allowing you to recognize when you are engaging in habits or activities that may be harmful to your mental or physical health. For example, if you notice that you are spending too much time on social media or engaging in other activities that are not contributing to your overall well-being, you can take steps to change these habits and replace them with healthier behaviors.

Overall, mindfulness can help you to become more aware of your thoughts, emotions, and behaviors, and allowing you to make positive changes in your life that can improve your mental health and overall well-being.

Enhanced Emotional Regulation: Mindfulness can help you regulate your emotions and allowing you to respond more calmly and thoughtfully to challenging situations.

Enhanced Emotional Regulation in parenting refers to the ability of parents to regulate their own emotions in a way that helps them respond more effectively to their children's needs and behaviors. Parenting can be challenging, and children can often push their parents' buttons, causing them to react emotionally.

However, when parents are able to regulate their emotions, they are better able to respond calmly and thoughtfully to their children, even in stressful situations.

Enhanced Emotional Regulation in parenting involves several key-skills, including:

- **Self-awareness**: This involves being aware of your own emotions and recognizing how they may impact your parenting. For example, if you are feeling stressed or overwhelmed, you may be more likely to snap at your child.

- **Emotional regulation:** This involves managing your own emotions in a way that helps you stay calm and focused. This may involve taking deep breaths, using relaxation techniques, or finding ways to distract yourself from negative emotions.

- **Empathy:** This involves understanding and connecting with your child's emotions, and responding in a way that is supportive and caring. For example, if your child is upset, you may offer a comforting hug or a listening ear.

- **Effective communication:** This involves expressing your own emotions in a clear and respectful way, and actively listening to your child's feelings and concerns. This can help you build a stronger relationship with your child and create a more positive and supportive home environment.

Overall, Enhanced Emotional Regulation in parenting can help parents be more responsive, nurturing, and supportive, which can have a positive impact on their children's emotional well-being and development.

Improved Relationships: Mindfulness can help improve communication and empathy, leading to better relationships with others.

Please remember, an improved relationship in parenting can refer to a situation where a parent and child have a closer, more positive and supportive bond. This type of relationship is characterized by effective communication, mutual respect, trust, and emotional support.

When parents have an improved relationship with their children, they are more likely to have a positive impact on their child's development, including their academic and social success, emotional well-being, and overall mental health. Improved parenting relationships can also lead to reduced behavioral problems and improved self-esteem in children.

One of the most important ways to improve the parent-child relationship is to establish a healthy and consistent communication channel. Parents who listen to their children with an open mind, validate their feelings and concerns, and provide them feedback that is constructive, supportive, and respectful can help build a positive and strong relationship.

Other ways to improve parenting relationships include spending quality time together, setting boundaries and expectations, providing discipline that is firm but fair, being a positive role model, and showing empathy and understanding towards their children's needs and struggles.

In summary, an improved relationship in parenting involves developing a supportive, positive, and respectful relationship between parent and child. This type of relationship is beneficial to the child's development, and can be achieved through effective communication, setting boundaries, providing discipline, being a positive role model, and showing empathy and understanding towards their child's needs.

When it comes to children, mindfulness can help with their personal growth in the following ways:

- **Improved Focus and Attention:** Mindfulness can help children improve their ability to focus and pay attention in school and other activities.

- **Enhanced Emotional Regulation:** Mindfulness can help children regulate their emotions, leading to better behavior and decision-making.

- **Increased Self-Awareness:** Mindfulness can help children become more aware of their thoughts, emotions, and behaviors, leading to increased self-confidence and self-esteem.

- **Improved Social Skills:** Mindfulness can help children develop better social skills, such as empathy and compassion, leading to stronger relationships with others.

- **Reduced Stress and Anxiety:** Mindfulness can help children reduce stress and anxiety, leading to a happier and more positive outlook on life.

Overall, practicing mindfulness can be beneficial for both adults and children, leading to personal growth and an improved the quality of life.

Chapter 12

CREATING A GROWTH-FOCUSED ENVIRONMENT

The importance of the environment in fostering growth and learning:

* *Strategies for creating a growth-focused home and community environment*

* *How to involve others (e.g., teachers, coaches) in creating a growth-focused environment*

"A child must know that he is a miracle, that since the beginning of the world, there hasn't been, and until the end of the world, there will not be, another child like him."

--Pablo Casals

Creating a growth-focused environment for your kid is essential for their overall development and success in life. Here are some tips to create such an environment:

I. **Encourage exploration and curiosity:** Allow your child to explore new things, try different activities, and ask questions. This will help them develop a growth mindset and a love for learning.

II. **Provide opportunities for learning:** Make sure your child has access to books, educational toys, and other learning materials that can help them develop new skills and knowledge.

III. **Emphasize effort over outcome:** Praise your child's effort rather than their achievements. This will help them understand that hard work and persistence are essential for success.

IV. **Set goals and track progress:** Help your child set achievable goals and track their progress towards them. Celebrate their achievements along the way and help them learn from their mistakes.

V. **Foster a positive attitude:** Encourage your child to have a positive attitude towards challenges and failures. Help them see failures as opportunities to learn and grow.

VI. **Provide a supportive and nurturing environment:** Create a safe and supportive environment where your child feels comfortable to take risks, try new things, and learn from their mistakes.

VII. **Be a role model:** Be a positive role model for your child by demonstrating a growth mindset, setting goals, and working towards achieving them.

By creating a growth-focused environment for your child, you can help them develop the skills and mindset they need to thrive and succeed in life.

Beliefs play a crucial role in shaping a child's resilience and confidence. Parents and caregivers can instill positive beliefs in their children from an early age, which can help them develop a growth mindset, optimism, and a sense of self-efficacy.

Some key beliefs that parents can help their children develop include the belief that mistakes are opportunities for learning and growth, that their abilities and skills can improve with practice and effort, and that setbacks and challenges are temporary and can be overcome.

Additionally, parents can model these beliefs through their own actions and attitudes. When children see their parents facing challenges with a positive attitude and working hard to overcome them, they are more likely to internalize these beliefs themselves.

Overall, instilling positive beliefs in children can help them develop the resilience and confidence they need to thrive in life, both academically and personally.

Instilling positive beliefs and values in children can have a positive impact on their development, including their ability to handle challenges, cope with stress, and build healthy relationships. Children who grow up with a strong sense of self-worth and confidence are more likely to be resilient in the face of adversity and more motivated to pursue their goals.

Positive beliefs can include messages like, "You are capable," "You can learn from mistakes," and "You are loved and valued." Children who internalize these messages are more likely to have a growth mindset and view challenges as opportunities for growth rather than as threats to their self-worth. This can lead to greater academic achievement and success in other areas of life.

However, it's important to note that instilling positive beliefs in children is not a guarantee of success or happiness. Children also need to develop skills and strategies for dealing with difficult situations, and they need supportive environments that allow them to thrive. Parents, caregivers, and educators can play a key role in creating these environments and supporting children's growth and development.

Finally, I want to end with a real-life story of a great actress whose beliefs turned into her achievement

Throughout her career, Viola Davis has been a vocal advocate for greater representation of women and people of colour in the entertainment industry. She has spoken out about the challenges of being a Black woman in Hollywood and the need for greater diversity in casting and storytelling.

Davis has also been open about her struggles with poverty and discrimination in her early life. She grew up in a family of sharecroppers in South Carolina and faced many obstacles in pursuing her dreams of acting.

Despite these challenges, Davis remained committed to her beliefs and her passion for acting. She worked tirelessly to hone her craft and build her career, earning critical acclaim and numerous awards along the way. In 2015, she became the first Black woman to win an Emmy Award for Outstanding Lead Actress in a Drama Series, and in 2017, she became the first Black actor to win the Triple Crown of Acting (an Oscar, an Emmy, and a Tony).

Through her hard work and dedication, Davis has not only achieved great success as an actress, but also helped to pave the way for greater diversity and representation in the entertainment industry. Her beliefs and values have been a driving force behind her achievements and serve as an inspiration to many.

By having faith in your child and cultivating their confidence, you may inspire them to become a remarkable individual who is content with their existence and capable of achieving limitless possibilities.

This means that when parents have confidence in their child's abilities and potential, and actively work to build their child's self-esteem and belief in themselves, they can have a significant impact on their child's future success and happiness.

When parents believe in their child's abilities, they can provide a positive and supportive environment that fosters their child's personal growth and development. This can help the child build confidence and self-esteem, which can empower them to pursue their dreams and overcome challenges.

When parents cultivate their child's confidence, they can inspire them to become more resilient, self-assured, and capable of achieving their goals. This, in turn, can help the child develop a sense of contentment with their existence and a positive outlook on life.

When children are raised with faith and confidence, they are more likely to take risks, pursue their passions, and explore new opportunities. They are also more likely to develop a sense of independence and self- reliance, which can lead to greater personal fulfilment and a higher level of achievement.

Overall, by having faith in their child and cultivating their confidence, parents can help their child become a remarkable individual capable of achieving limitless possibilities, which can lead to a happy and fulfilling life.

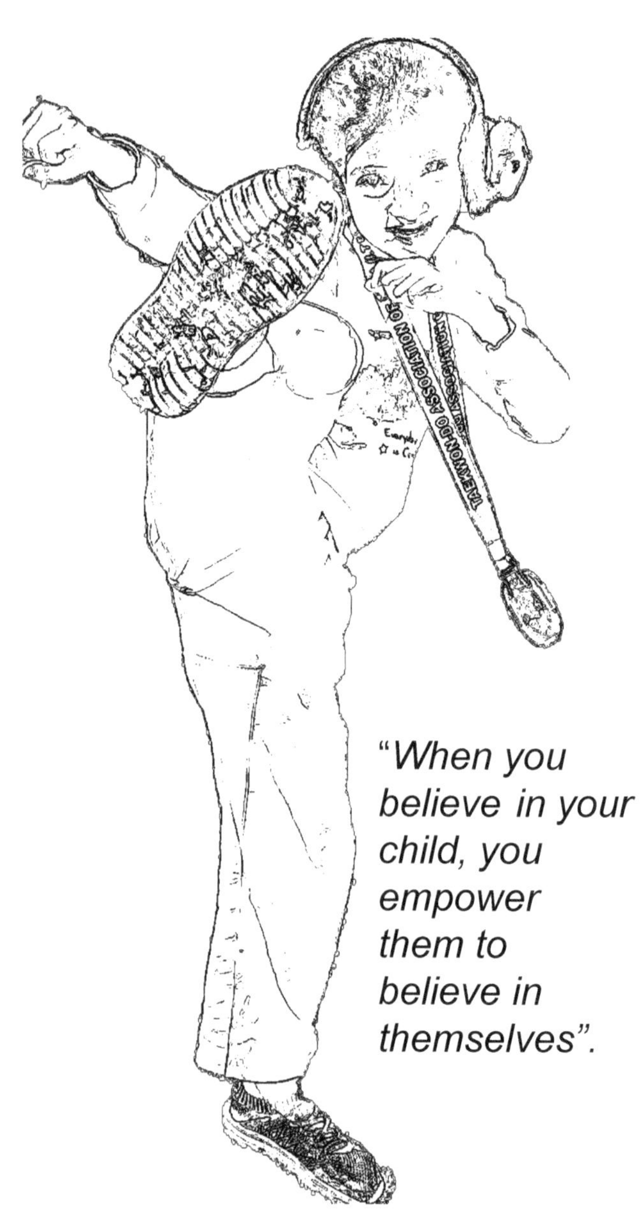

"When you believe in your child, you empower them to believe in themselves".

As parents, we want the best for our children. We want them to grow up to be confident, capable, and successful individuals. But sometimes, we may underestimate the power of our support and belief in our children. When we believe in our kids, it can have a tremendous impact on their development and overall well-being.

Believing in your kid means having faith in their abilities, encouraging them to pursue their dreams, and being their biggest cheerleader. It means acknowledging their strengths and weaknesses and helping them develop the skills they need to succeed. When children feel like their parents believe in them, they are more likely to take risks, set goals, and work towards achieving them.

It can have a lasting impact on their self-esteem, confidence, and motivation. Children who feel supported by their parents are more likely to take on challenges, set goals, and work towards achieving them. So, let your child know that you believe in them and that you are there to support them every step of the way.

Thank you!

You can connect with me at:

 *advocate.sandigdhamishra@gmail.com*
advsandigdha@paydirtprofessionals.com

 *linkedin.com/in/sandigdhamishra*

 *facebook.com/paydirtprofessionals*

Follow on Instagram

@ADVOCATE.SANDIGDHAMISHRA

Paydirt Professionals

 *paydirtprofessionals.com*